LEATHERSTOCKING
GHOSTS

HAUNTED PLACES IN CENTRAL NEW YORK

LYNDA LEE MACKEN

LEATHERSTOCKING GHOSTS

ISBN 0-9755244-2-9

Cover design:
Debra Tremper
Six Penny Graphics, Fredericksburg, VA

Cover photo:
Woodland Cemetery Gate
Delhi, New York

Back cover logo design:
Glenda Moore, catStuff Graphics

Printed on recycled paper by
Sheridan Books, Ann Arbor, MI

CONTENTS

A spooky regional tale intended to scare children away from rivers relates to the spirit of an Iroquois woman who eternally searches the Susquehanna River for her drowned children; she'll snatch away any child who walks too near the water.

INTRODUCTION

New York's heartland is rife with ghosts and tales of hauntings. Spirits skulk about burial grounds, supernatural strains of piano music resound, and some specters strike out in a bowling hall. Such are the haunted happenings in Central New York.

Populated with phantoms of those who helped shape the region, Cooperstown, Herkimer, Oriskany, Rome and Syracuse are some of the places where influential and heroic spirits still reside. Trapped in time, for reasons unknown, their ethereal presence bears witness to long-gone eras.

Cooperstown is described as "America's most perfect village." But beneath its charming façade lurks a long list of resident ghosts. Founded in 1786 by William Cooper, the spooky goings-on in the idyllic village were first chronicled in 1921. Since then, more wraiths have taken up residence in the picturesque town - who can blame them.

Opulent manors reflect the wealth of foresighted entrepreneurs who made their fortunes in the region. Parke Avery, George Clark, Clark Dodge, and Alonzo Roberson's grand palaces possess a denizen or two, which adds a chilly chapter to their success stories.

The Mohawk Valley suffered grave losses during the French and Indian War and American Revolution. First inhabited by Native Americans, supernatural stories of their tribes are legendary. Faithful ghosts carry on expressing their spirits in myriad ways at Indian Castle Church, Forts Klock, Stanwix, and Herkimer Church.

Syracuse boasts a bevy of haunted locations. Its landmark City Hall is one of several spirited sites in "Salt City." Strange that a place with so much saline has so many ghosts since salt is said to keep the spooks away!

Remarkably, some places overflow with otherworldly oddities like O'Connor's Alexander Hamilton Inn in Clinton where the spirit of a little girl is joined by a host of other ghosts. Even the Wayside Inn in Elbridge exudes eerie, ephemeral presences.

The true nature of ghosts and hauntings remains a mystery, but an ancient belief suggests an explanation. In some cases the conscious and unconscious split at the time of death. The "soul" goes on to reincarnate while its lifeless counterpart, or spirit, remains trapped in an eternal trance of its own memories and feelings, unaware, and unable to communicate and reason.

In most cases, ghost behavior does resemble the primal notion of an ethereal, unconscious intelligence trapped in time due to the loss of its conscious half.

Still, the paranormal continues to captivate all who encounter spirits, and hopefully, all who read about them.

So dear reader, enjoy an unearthly journey through eerie forts, spirited inns, and possessed museums. Uncover the buried secrets of battlefields and B & Bs. Learn to love *paranormal* New York as revealed on the pages of *Leatherstocking Ghosts*.

ALONZO ROBERSON MANSION
Binghamton

In 1904, astute businessman and craftsman Alonzo Roberson Jr. married local schoolteacher Margaret Hays. The Binghamton natives built an Italian Renaissance Revival style manse downtown on prestigious Front Street. Their estate comprised a main house, carriage house, greenhouse and pergola with gardens, and boasted an opulent interior with every modern amenity - including an elevator.

Community oriented, Alonzo served as president of the Roberson & Son Lumber Company and Chairman of Marine Midland Bank. The charitable duo supported many causes they believed in, but shied away from the spotlight.

After Alonzo Jr. died in 1934, house servants reported seeing his apparition riding in the mansion's elevator.

When Margaret passed away 20 years later, Alonzo's will bequeathed the estate to the community for use as an educational center. The Roberson Center opened in 1954.

Are the spirits of the philanthropic couple still watching over their mansion? Tours aimed at raising funds for the museum, told of late night, ghostly organ music filtering through the dwelling, unexplainable noises, and the sound of disembodied footsteps.

Could Clark Dodge or Walter Pratt be the phantom who appeared in his former home at Christmastime?

DODGE-PRATT-NORTHAM CENTER
Boonville

Prominent Boonville banker and druggist Clark Dodge built the ornate mansion at 106 Schuyler Street in the 1800s. The architectural landmark, which contains Italian marble fireplaces, Tiffany windows, crystal chandeliers and gold leaf, is considered one of the finest regional examples of French Second Empire architecture, a style popular in the late 19th century.

Listed on the National Register of Historic Places and named for the three families who previously owned the house, the last owner, Hazel Northam, a New York City undertaker, summered there and bequeathed the mansion in 1972 to the adjacent Erwin Library.

The non-profit center hosts art shows, concerts, classes, community and ghostly gatherings.

Several years ago, as staffer Sue Ulrich decorated the Christmas tree, she definitely felt someone watching her. Turning around, she observed an older gent dressed casually in slacks, a sweater and carpet slippers staring at her. The fully formed apparition appeared "solid" like any other human being and his face expressed the question, "What are *you* doing here?"

Ms. Ulrich just went back to work and since then has not had any more spectral visitations, most likely because she doesn't want to!

SOUTH COTTAGE
Cazenovia

In 1968, the New York State Historic Trust took title to a rare "find," an architecturally significant building with intact furnishings and collections that spanned five generations.

The Lorenzo State Historic Site at 17 Rippleton Road originated with Dutch naval officer John Lincklaen's arrival at Cazenovia Lake in 1792.

By 1803 the prospering agent for the Holland Land Company envisioned a grand home with expansive views at the south end of the lake. Five years later, his dream came true.

In the 1940s, relation George Ledyard, Jr. and his wife Annie retired to Cazenovia. They resided in South Cottage, a guesthouse built in the early 19th century.

After the couple died, (Annie passed away in the house), family friends resided in South Cottage. It appears that an ancestral member didn't approve of a non-relative living there.

Doors flew open, books flew off tables, and even apparitions plagued the tenants. An awesome spectral figure sat in a rocking chair by the fire, smoking a pipe. His appearance ended speculation that Annie was their resident ghost.

Lorenzo is a survivor of a centuries old summer colony and its guest cottage now shelters office workers who thankfully aren't bothered by any ghosts.

WILLOWBANK
Cazenovia

Perhaps it's the home's proximity to the water, a common component in hauntings, or maybe it's the character of the household that allowed another family related property on Cazenovia Lake to retain the spirit of a former occupant.

When Sydney and Helen Fairchild lived at Willowbank, Mrs. Fairchild customarily enjoyed a cup of afternoon tea as she stitched her needlework. A loyal servant, whose name has been lost to history, always ensured the lady of the house sipped her spot of tea on the dot.

The prompt and faithful servant kept her routine way beyond her required years and continued her service from the other side.

For years after the maid's death, Helen Fairchild heard the clatter of delicate china being carried on a tray down the stairs just as she did every day when her loyal servant was alive. Sometimes she felt a cool hand on her shoulder, the maid's way of showing affection toward her employer in life.

Subsequent owners never experienced the maid's presence so we can only assume that her spirit is now attending Mrs. Fairchild in the great beyond.

(Photo courtesy Clinton Historical Society.)

At O'Connor's Alexander Hamilton inn, a female apparition lingers on the second floor; a spectral young girl spins circles in the kitchen, and yet another little girl's ghost descends the stairs to peer into the dining room.

O'CONNOR'S ALEXANDER HAMILTON INN
Clinton

Early on at O'Connor's Alexander Hamilton Inn, Chef Robert J. Sterling heard something in the cellar and went down to investigate the noise. He noticed that someone forgot to shut the light, but suddenly that light came toward him and passed through his body flooding Sterling with a tingling sensation.

Shaken, he raced upstairs and spent the better part of the next day recovering from the terrifying incident.

Days later he observed the light in the cellar again, but this time the glow clearly revealed the figure of a little girl. Since then the chef sees the spectral youngster at least once a week peering through doorways, among other places.

Central New York Ghost Hunter Society investigators even captured the chilling voice of the little girl on audiotape saying, "I'm here, I'm here." The tiny voice, faint and low, responded to a ghost surveyor who explained the tape recording device to any unseen entities, why the investigators were there, and asked if the spirits had anything to say.

According to owner Patrick O'Connor, who opened the inn at 21 West Park Row in 1999, lawyer Othniel Williams built the brick structure between 1826 and 1832. The residence stayed in Williams' family until 1938 when it was sold to a Utica lawyer. Opened as Ade's Hotel in 1942 and in 1946 as the Alexander Hamilton

Inn, the old hostelry hosts several active spirits who are totally harmless and a bother to no one. Staffers and patrons encounter unearthly beings but feel totally at-ease with their otherworldly associates.

One persistent sighting is of a middle-aged man in work clothes who hangs around the property. Could this wraith, whom they call "George," be a former groundskeeper?

A female apparition lingers on the second floor; a spectral young girl spins circles in the kitchen, and yet another little girl ghost descends the stairs to peer into the dining room.

Psychics feel that the original family entertained regularly due to their social standing. During that era the little girl would be sent to bed, but some time later she'd come down the stairs and peek through the French doors to watch the festivities.

O'Connor, who lives at the inn, witnessed the ghostly girl descend the stairs while speaking with one of his workers. Their eyes met and her wraith smiled at him. Reaching the bottom of the stairs, she walked into the living room and disappeared...

Other odd happenings at the inn include wine glasses that move by themselves and mops that travel from place to place. Quite often, windows are found open in guest rooms after housekeeping has tidied up and locked the room.

These days Chef Sterling says he looks forward to seeing the little girl in the early mornings. Although initially frightened by her presence, he now enjoys her company. So far she hasn't communicated with him even though he talks to her - she just waves and smiles.

BULL'S HEAD INN
Cobleskill

The oldest building in the village of Cobleskill is also its most haunted. The Bull's Head Inn opened to the public in 1802 but forty years later became a private residence.

In 1966 when it again opened as a restaurant, silverware, plates, and napkins started flying about. When the apparition of a woman in white showed up in the previous resident's bedroom, Mrs. John Stacy turned out to be the obvious culprit.

Mrs. Stacy lived in the Federal Georgian style house at 2 Park Place from 1920 to 1966. A woman of self-restraint, and loyal member of the Women's Christian Temperance Union, most agree her displeasure with drinking stems from her days with Mr. Stacy who tippled a little too much.

Seeing strangers guzzle in her former home gets Stacy's ghost going. Captain's chairs swivel without explanation and an old crank phone, that's disconnected, will sometimes ring.

While dining, a couple sat dumbfounded as a plate lifted off their table and flew across the room. Workers claim to see a shadowy shape and a vague figure in mirrors. After closing, one worker observed Stacy's ethereal form floating behind the bar.

Most times the creepiness intensifies when late night revelers are reluctant to leave the old-time watering hole.

JOHN MILLER HOUSE
Cooperstown

Anyone on Bruce Markusen's Candlelight Ghost Tour will hear the chilling tale of the John Miller house.

Miller built the red brick structure at the southwest corner of Lake Street and Pine Boulevard in 1802. Originally constructed as a farmhouse, it is the oldest brick home in Cooperstown.

According to legend, when an unknown couple lived there a terrible murder took place.

The story goes that the farmer found his wife unbearable. She had driven him to the brink of insanity and he could see only one way out of the madness...

One night he silently crept into the bedroom, stealthily picked up a pillow, placed it over her face, and smothered her to death.

They say that in the still of the night, muffled moaning sounds sometimes emanate from the house. On occasion, disembodied screams pierce the silence in the usually tranquil neighborhood.

Is the farmer's wife struggle imprinted on the environment? Perhaps her desperate spirit is stuck in an eternal loop that replays her final moments over and over.

THE OLD STONE WALL
Cooperstown

James Fenimore Cooper speculates that the ghosts of the village founded by his great-grandfather cling to the old part of the town because the river binds them there, for legend says ghosts and witches cannot cross water.

River Street is legendary for its stories of ghosts and haunted homes. Cooperstown's oldest ghost story is the one about the Indian chief "who for nearly a century and a half is known to have sat behind the old stonewall on River Street, and with his sturdy, if bony legs, many a time kicked it down."[1]

For generations the story passed on that in back of the wall sat the skeleton of a great Mohawk Chief with "chin on knees and hands clasped around shinbones amidst his weapons and scanty pots and pipes."[2]

Although the ornery Chief never left his grave, no wall ever stood, or ever would stand, at that place. Wall after wall went up and ended up kicked down by the immortal Chief, until the present one, thick and strong enough to withstand his pushing.

According to Cooper, if the wall ever falls again, the triumphant old chief with ghastly eyes and skinny legs will still be there gloating over his victory.

---

[1] James Fenimore Cooper. *The Legends and Traditions of a Northern County*, page 36.
[2] Ibid, page 37.

Ann Cooper's ghost, at the time still living in her mortal abode, helped a confused traveler find his way.

POMEROY PLACE
Cooperstown

The first stone house constructed in the village was Pomeroy Place built by Judge William Cooper as a wedding gift to his daughter Ann and her husband, George Pomeroy.

The house at the corner of Main and River Streets is unusual because the stonework is laid in a herringbone pattern, which makes the house unique. The year of construction and the couple's initials were added to the stone design symbolically cementing their union.

The couple lived happily for many years and raised ten children. In fact, Ann felt so contented in her earthly abode that she may have never left.

One rainy night, a minister stopped at the property to ask directions to the rector's house. After knocking repeatedly, the heavy door creaked open and a little old lady in black holding a candle pointed out the way.

The cleric shared his tale with his host who stated that couldn't be - the house stood vacant. The guest insisted, so the two men agreed to settle the issue by going over to the house.

The visitor led the way and admitted that it did look deserted. He knocked and pounded, but no lady appeared. They agreed the incident was baffling and affirmed that even Cooperstown *ghosts* are friendly.

Not only that, passersby often claimed to see Ann's face peering out the windowpanes.

Another Cooper ghost supposedly remained in "Greencrest" as well as the spirit of an Indian Chief.

GREENCREST
Cooperstown

Two ghosts reputedly haunt the house located on River Street directly behind Ann Cooper's home. Known as "Greencrest," James Fenimore Cooper's grandson and namesake originally chronicled the hauntings at the Victorian dwelling in *The Legends and Traditions of a Northern County.*

It's another Cooper ghost that supposedly remained in the house as well as the spirit of an Indian Chief whose grave is said to be on the property.

John Worthington built the house in 1873 for he and his wife Jenny Cooper.

They say that when the couple married, Jenny gave her husband a portrait of her as a wedding gift. Their marriage ended suddenly, however, because Jenny died shortly after at the age of 18.

When John remarried, he removed Jenny's portrait because his new wife wanted the painting taken down.

That's when his bad luck began. John got spooked and quickly reattached the painting to the wall.

The word on the street is that Jenny's portrait still hangs inside her mortal domain.

Stories circulated that a ghostly figure seemed to rise from Christ Church burial ground and move slowly about.

More River Street Haunts
Cooperstown

Byberry Cottage was home to the novelist's daughter Susan Fenimore Cooper. A dyed in the wool altruist, Susan founded a hospital, orphanage, and the "Home for Old Women." Although nearly deaf, the delicate woman possessed an extraordinary gift.

As a mentalist, she performed levitation for her friends and relatives with no object too heavy to move. She frequently demonstrated this talent by lifting an inverted dining table that held a corpulent man seated on a pile of books.

Deeply religious, a few years before her death, she received a message from the spirits who warned her gift was of the devil. She refused to practice ever again.

Another River Street ghost is the very last occupant of Ms. Cooper's Byberry Cottage. Blind, and with only one leg, the invalid woman who resided there lived in a wheel chair. Totally devoted, she looked forward to attending services at her beloved Christ Church. When weather permitted, her nurse pushed her in the chair to church on Sundays.

During Good Friday service, a congregation member, who possessed the "sixth sense," watched with amazement as the wheel chair with its invalid occupant moved *on its own* up the middle aisle of the church!

Normally the nurse turned the wheelchair sideways when it reached the transepts where it stood during services, but on this Good Friday, the chair moved somberly up through the choir and vanished into thin air when it reached the altar.

When the service ended, the preacher announced that the invalid had died shortly before.

Cooper provides another ghostly tale in his legendary book.

Like Judge Cooper, James Averell, Jr. and his son, William Holt Averell, influenced Cooperstown and Otsego County through much of the 19th century.

Son William, an ambitious lawyer, helped settle William Cooper's estate. In fact, he made a fortune by buying Cooper properties as they came to market.

The last of the "old colored body servants," Black Dick looked after Master Avery in his declining years making life easy for him.

When Averell died and was buried in Christ Church graveyard, Dick grieved terribly and was heartbroken.

Stories soon circulated that a ghostly figure seemed to rise from the church's burial ground and move slowly about as if in a daze. Many townspeople, who carried candle-lit lanterns to light their way after dark, steered clear of the graveyard.

The ghost sightings became so prevalent that a few brave souls decided to spend a night among the graves to watch for the phantom.

 Sure enough, eventually a shadowy figure arose and moved about old Averell's grave. After the witnesses regained their composure, they approached the specter and laid bare the interloper - old Black Dick.

The ever-faithful servant skulked nightly to his master's grave to watch and mourn over it.

The loss so severely disturbed the black man's mind that he followed Master Averell to the next life soon thereafter.

There's another shadowy visitor who used to be seen in the old house that formerly stood opposite the Indians' grave on River Street.

James Fenimore Cooper's grandson recalled his childhood visits to the home of his deceased uncle to see his cousin.

Once time he took a seat in Richard Fenimore Cooper's library chair only to be vigorously admonished not to sit there because his dead uncle occupied it!

Cooper maintained that he forever internalized this event as well as *all* the other "terrors" of River Street.

"The spirit of Leatherstocking surely haunts the happy hunting grounds of the woods and lake of Otsego."

- James Fenimore Cooper (1858-1938)
The Legends and Traditions of a Northern County

A ghostly wail emanates from The Smithy.

THE SMITHY
Cooperstown

55 Pioneer Street is the oldest building in Cooperstown. Judge William Cooper built the place in 1786 as a blacksmith shop and a storage facility for the growing settlement.

In 1927, Marguerite Standish Cockett and Marjorie Jackson converted its first floor, the oldest part of the building, into an antique shop. Later the stone constructed ground floor became a pottery studio.

The pottery studio is active again at The Smithy-Pioneer Gallery where the works of contemporary local artists are on display. Also exhibited are vestiges of the old blacksmith shop - forges, anvil stands, and smoke-shadows of horseshoes.

Another remnant of its long history is the mysterious wailing that sometimes emanates from the place during the night.

There is no clue as to who the ghostly howler might be since there is no record of someone dying here. Skeptics say the ungodly noise probably has something to do with revelers at the nearby taverns.

The specter of an older woman at the Tunnicliff Inn may be its former owner.

TUNNICLIFF INN
Cooperstown

The Tunnicliff Inn at 34-36 Pioneer Street is one of the oldest brick structures in the village. Erected in 1802 by Lawrence McNamee as a General Store, 36 years later the building re-opened as the American Hotel.

Lester Tunnicliff purchased the place in 1916 and renamed the hotel the Tunnicliff Inn. Ten years later, John J. Frank and his sister Magdalene became owners.

The Tunnicliff Inn received the first liquor license in the town following the repeal of the Prohibition Act.

Frank excavated the Tap Room level and opened "The Home Plate" to coincide with the opening of the National Baseball Hall of Fame and Museum in 1939. Because of its underground local, the Home Plate eventually became known as "The Pit," one of the oldest establishments in town still featuring its original bar.

In 1975 over 300 people attended an open house at the inn given by Magdalene Frank to mark her 50th anniversary as owner of the popular Cooperstown hotel.

Staffer Mike Henrici lives at the inn and has awakened several times to see the specter of an older woman standing in his room. He strongly suspects the apparition is Magdalene.

Several guests have shared the same experience.

Most likely Magdalene doesn't realize she's dead; she probably wants another party to commemorate her 80th year at the place.

The Overlook B & B is a special place and its former owner remains an extraordinary part of it.

Overlook Bed and Breakfast
Cooperstown

During World War II, Cooperstown resident, Minnie Marsh White, wanted to take a road trip to Florida. Unfortunately gas rationing prohibited the journey. The story goes that the affluent woman committed suicide by hanging herself in her attic because she couldn't go.

Gayle and Jack Smith have operated the Overlook Bed and Breakfast, Minnie's sprawling Victorian home, for nearly 20 years. They claim that the woman's spirit is very friendly and most guests say they sense her presence. Although Minnie's specter has never appeared, her spirit manifests in subtle, and sometimes obvious, ways.

Alone in the house, Gayle once heard classical music playing while tidying up the sunroom.

When the owners decorated the walls with photographs and historical documents about Minnie, the long gone matriarch made a ruckus. While guests were relaxing in the living room after supper, a loud crash came from the kitchen. Gayle raced to investigate and found a large, heavy cooking pan on the floor. No way could the pot have moved off the counter by itself.

Yes, Minnie occasionally makes noises and lifts things from time to time, (she always returns the objects); life goes on peacefully at the pleasant inn.

The Overlook B & B at 8 Pine Boulevard is a special place and Minnie remains an extraordinary part of it.

The Otesaga - where ghosts are known to whisper names.

THE OTESAGA
Cooperstown

"Otesaga" is the Iroquois word for meeting place and at this "grand dame" of a resort unseen sociable spirits gather at the Glimmerglass Bar & Lounge.

Since 1909 the imposing Federal-style structure has welcomed guests to the southern shore of Lake Otsego. In this case, it seems one or two guests, and a group of obnoxious children have stayed way past check out time.

Bartender, Rachel Purcell shared that at least three times a year she hears her name clearly called. When she alertly responds, no one is there. The culprit is a woman whose voice is soft and even-toned. Once, however, a male voice summoned her.

This anomaly usually occurs at dusk near the dining room by the veranda and is accompanied by a cold chill. Rachel is not the only one who hears the voice - three cocktail waitresses heard the whisperer call their names.

Another co-worker approached a guest from behind to ask if she could bring him anything. Her eyes diverted briefly to pull the order book from her apron, but by the time she reached the rocking chair the guest was gone even though she had observed his arm resting on the chair not a second before.

On two occasions guests called the front desk late at night to complain about errant children running up and down the hallway. A small army of clerks investigated every floor but the spectral kids could not be caught.

*High on the hill behind the Farmer's Museum rests an ancient
Seneca log house with a haunting history.*

SENECA LOG HOUSE
Cooperstown

The Farmer's Museum is located 1 mile north of the village of Cooperstown on State Route 80 on the west side of Otsego Lake.

The site is deeply rooted in New York's rural past. The land has been part of a working farm since 1813, when James Fenimore Cooper owned it. Known as Fenimore Farm since 1829, the property changed hands when the Clark family acquired it in the 1870s.

High on the hill behind the museum rests an ancient Seneca log house with an unusual history.

Originally constructed during the American Revolution on what is now the Tonawanda Reservation near Buffalo, the log house is comprised of one rectangular room with a loft above. Historian Dave Rickard contends that the structure was probably built by British troops from Fort Niagara as housing for loyalist Indians.

In the early 1930s, the City of Rochester purchased the log dwelling and used it as a tourist information booth eventually altering the diminutive house to represent the area's first white settlers' cabin.

About 20 years later, a Pittsford resident bought it for twenty-five dollars and his kids enjoyed it as a playhouse. The historic Native American log house stood in his backyard for the next forty years.

In the late 1990s, the New York State Historical Association searched for a log Indian dwelling to enhance the Farmer's Museum. Finally the shifting structure found a permanent home in Cooperstown.

The NYSHA spent over two years researching the history of the house. Archival photographs showed the log home standing on the Tonawanda Reservation in the 1930s. When Rickard showed the pictures to some of the reservation's oldest residents, one of them gasped. "You have the house!" she whispered.[3]

Little Beard, a Seneca who fought against the patriots, initially owned the house. In retaliation, American forces burned down many Iroquois villages, but British troops came to the aid of their allies by constructing log houses for the loyalists.[4]

Upon Little Beard's death, the house passed to his daughter, Harriet Little Beard Clute, then down through several more generations until 1930 when a descendant named Phoebe Fish Sundown lived in the log home with her two sons. That's when the trouble began.

Phoebe's older son Henry confronted an old crone who lived nearby. The tribe ostracized the woman because she practiced black magic. The boy taunted her until she looked daggers at him and carved his image on a tree depicting his death.

Henry went home and told his mother he wanted to shoot at crows in the backyard but instead removed a pistol from a drawer and shot himself in the head.

---

[3] Jim Atwell, "A story of portable ghosts." *The Cooperstown Crier.*
[4] The burning of Indian villages began at Cooperstown.

Younger son Montville blamed the wizened woman for his brother's death and threatened her. Again, she carved a death scene on a tree trunk. Montville went home and hanged himself from a beam inside the house.

When Phoebe herself challenged the witch, promising to avenge her sons' deaths, "You too shall die," replied the awful woman.

Soon thereafter as Phoebe lay in bed, a former lover shot her to death with the same revolver that killed her oldest son. Then her murderer turned the gun on himself.

Three suicides and a murder all took place in the tiny log dwelling.

The Seneca believe that Phoebe passed on to the afterlife but the three suicide victims are "stuck" in this realm, forever trapped in the small log house. Tribesmen believe the three men's spirits have traveled with that house through all its moves across New York State and dwell in it yet, in Cooperstown.

Before the Seneca log house opened to the public in 1999, a Seneca shaman conducted an "Okewa," a ceremony meant to assist the dead on their journey to the next world. When it comes to suicides, all the rite can do is allay the spirits and help them to accept their fate.

Every year, Senecas return to Cooperstown to repeat the Okewa, staying in touch with three tribal brothers dead eighty-five years.

In 1800, when Ann Cooper Clarke was evicted from Hyde Hall, she threatened to return and haunt it forever.

HYDE HALL
Cooperstown

When her thankless children evicted Ann Cooper Clarke from her house in 1800, she threatened to return and haunt it forever.

The aristocratic Clarke family's lengthy residence at Hyde Hall provides a remarkable record of over 250 years of New York State history and almost certainly guarantees a legacy of spirits left behind to inhabit the ancestral home.

George Clarke inherited his proper English family's vast real estate holdings (120,000 acres) and sugar cane fortune from Jamaican plantations, and commissioned the construction of a magnificent estate on a western hillside overlooking Otsego Lake.

Philip Hooker, a leading New York architect, designed the impressive showplace that today is considered the finest example of neoclassic country mansions anywhere in America. Hyde is composed of four structures, containing 50 rooms that enclose an open courtyard. This design set the structure apart from other American dwellings.

Clarke divorced his wife in 1813 (she refused to come to America) and married Ann Corey Cooper, the widow of James Fenimore Cooper's brother. When he died in 1835, he left his mansion and a portion of his fortune to his son George Clarke, Jr.

George Jr., a debonair young man, invested in risky enterprises. When the hops market collapsed in the late 19th century, George Jr. lost his investment and then some. He filed bankruptcy and relinquished the mansion.

George Jr.'s son, George Hyde Clarke, married into the Averell Carter family and his mother-in-law bought back the grand home and all of its contents.

Hyde Hall sheltered Clarke and his descendants for three generations and stands as a reminder of an era when British nobility created great estates in the former colonies.[5] The Clarke family is one of the few who managed to hold on to their assets during the tumult of the American Revolution.

New York State acquired the 3,000-acre property in 1963 for the development of Glimmerglass State Park. Time and lack of maintenance had taken their toll on the building and the state had no resources for restoration. The grand home faced demolition.

Fortunately "Friends of Hyde Hall" took charge and saved the house. In 1988, the non-profit organization gained full responsibility for the structure's restoration and management.

Visitors who tour the structure today can observe the faithful restoration in progress and they may also sense a presence from the past.

In *Ghosts of the Northeast*, author David Pitkin says the last remaining Clarkes asserted that their Alsatian dog refused to go down a rear stairway and snarled as if warding off an unwanted intruder. Often the sound of

---

[5] www.hydehall.org

disembodied footsteps resounded on this staircase as well as the main staircase outside the billiard room.

Pitkin explored the house, along with an intuitive friend, and gained a unique paranormal perspective. The sensitive discerned the imprints of a festive Christmas celebration, lively political discussions in the library, and the image of a young woman concerned about the welfare of a soldier fighting the Civil War (two Clarke family members died in the war between the states).

Workers renovating the house spied a dusty cloud take on an ethereal form and "swoosh" up a hallway. Speculation has it that the wraith may be the spirit of Arthur Sherwood, a family friend who died of heart failure in the house.

In 1921, James Fenimore Cooper's grandson and namesake initially recorded the hauntings of Hyde Hall in *The Legends and Traditions of a Northern County.*

Cooper, staying overnight in the blue room, claimed to see the specter of an older man. When he shared his experience with his hostess the next morning, she concurred that ghosts did appear in this little used room, once the sleeping quarters of George Clarke.

The frequently sighted specter dressed in a yellow, red, and green "wrapper," would walk down the hall and enter his former bedroom. Since Clarke's colorful robe lay folded in a household trunk, the family felt certain the ancestor haunted the premises.

Cooper wanted to believe the wraith was old Ann keeping her solemn oath to haunt the place forever - a promise she made nearly a century before when ordered from her home.

A passageway goes from inside the house to the family burial vault making it easy for the dead to easily pass to and fro.

Other spooky tales of the old house persist. In the dead of night, lively piano music is said to resonate from the gigantic drawing room.

When a family member died, he or she didn't have far to go to find a new resting place because the family crypt is built into the hillside just steps from the front door. An underground passageway goes from inside the house to the family burial vault making it easy for the dead to easily pass to and fro unnoticed and sheltered from the elements.

In the catacomb lay the stone sarcophagi of George Clarke and some family members. Cooper writes that years ago the burial chamber lay open to the living *and* the dead. The doors at each end of the passageway that led into the hillside tomb were kept unlocked providing easy access for the courageous, the curious, and the creepy.

The Inn at Hickory Grove has an energy all its own.

THE INN AT HICKORY GROVE
Cooperstown

Marie Curpier knew the moment she walked through the door of the circa 1830 Greek revival home that the inn was haunted.

As a prospective buyer in September 1998, Marie felt strange passing through the house that stood frozen in time. Keys, a grocery list, and clothing - all were left in place as if the owner had just gone out for a walk and would return any moment. In this case, they never did come back, abandoning the property in the middle of the night.

But Marie returned the next day, in fact, to re-inspect the site. Armed with a flashlight, since there was no power in the house, she made her rounds with the realtor. This time however, as the sun set behind the autumn hills, the place felt "different."

Out of the blue a phone started ringing somewhere in the enormous house. The realtor picked up the "Princess" phone and the caller asked for a person who the saleswoman knew lived up the street so informed them they had the wrong number and hung up. That's when Marie reminded the realtor that the phone was disconnected. The realtor removed the receiver from its cradle to double check - the phone was dead.

Marie is a sensitive person and picks up on things that others may not perceive and sensed the house screaming at her to *"Please open me back up!"*

The Curpiers moved in before the electricity was activated so when the new innkeeper wanted to look through some forsaken boxes, she stood near an open door to get more light. Actually, Marie had an ulterior motive; she wanted to be close to an exit just in case she needed to make a quick getaway.

As she sorted out the boxes she felt "something" walk by her and clearly heard a man clear his throat. She left the house for the rest of the day.

The Hickory Grove Inn, at 6855 State Highway 80, overlooks Otsego Lake and enjoyed popularity as a seasonal restaurant and bar for decades. One day as Marie walked through the commercial kitchen, she heard the walk-in cooler running and saw the red light illuminated signaling the machine's power was on. Shaken, she called her husband who assured her it was just an errant circuit breaker. *"But we have no electricity!"* She was barely able to get the words out. That was another day spent away from the residence.

One time a man appeared with his little boy to rent a room. For some reason Marie felt ill at ease with the prospective guest. As she showed the visitor Room 3 she discerned a voice saying, *"Turn around, turn around. Get out of the room."*

The next morning at breakfast, the guest wanted to know "what" was in his room. He described the sensation as a "strong presence" and commented that as he tried to shower the water kept shutting off, yet his son had no problem. That was the only time the shower acted up. Apparently, the spirits of the house didn't take kindly to the guest.

Marie feels certain the house protects her.

The spirits reacted violently to the invasion of ghost hunters who investigated the structure. Marie wasn't keen on their energy either and finally asked them to curtail their inspection and leave.

That night Marie and her husband awoke to a cacophony of jarring noises resounding downstairs in the kitchen; the racket sounded as if the place was being turned upside down and the couple was certain burglars ransacked their home

To their utter amazement, the place remained in perfect order and no one was in the house. Whoever, or whatever, created such a raucous disturbance for 45 minutes sent the pair packing to a hotel for the night and made them rethink their role as innkeepers.

The couple nearly sold their charming house with wood-beamed ceilings and fieldstone fireplace, but when the deal fell through Marie considered it a sign that reinforced their commitment to stick with the business.

Marie gave birth to a little girl and asked the spirits to tone it down because of the baby. They respected her wishes, although when their child turned two, the toddler's presence brought out the entity of a little girl who they hear whimpering next to their bed in the middle of the night on occasion.

Originally the inn functioned as a family farmstead that spanned five generations; the small cemetery on the hill behind the house holds the headstones of thirteen children. Perhaps this little invisible child is one of the deceased who doesn't realize she's dead.

Marie describes the energy in her home as the "spirit of the place" and doesn't feel that it's a specific entity.

Perhaps the force projected in the house harkens back to the Native Americans who originally occupied the site.

The inn exudes a dynamism all its own and likes being lived in. When open for business the atmosphere is calm and idyllic, but as soon as the Curpiers close for the season the house assumes a heavy, brooding mood.

That's when all manner of paranormal activity commences - doors slam, the sound of a ball bouncing or a noise like coins dropping and rolling on the floor is heard, the washer fills with water, the scent of perfume or the smell of a wet dog is perceived, - just about "anything and everything" has happened.

The couple renovated the property themselves and to this day tools remain missing. Hammers, saws, "you name it," disappeared, presumably taken by the spirit who is probably very busy on the other side.

The Curpiers' Himalayan cat has an odd habit of sitting under their armoire for hours on end staring at the wall. Originally a closet stood there but the couple walled it over and opened it on the other side creating a linen closet in the master bath.

Marie encountered a prior owner one day who cryptically told her, "The closet. You need to put it back. It lives there."

You'll be received with open arms at the Inn at Hickory Grove where the Curpiers, and the spirits, will be very happy you stayed.

*"I never have seen a haunted house, but I hear there are
such things;
That they hold the talk of spirits, their mirth and
sorrowings.
I know this house isn't haunted, and I wish it were, I do;
For it wouldn't be so lonely if it had a ghost or two."*

- Joyce Kilmer

from

The House with Nobody in It

WAYSIDE INN
Elbridge

At the turn of the 20th century, Harry Monroe mysteriously fell to his death down the basement well in the Wayside Inn. Supposedly, his fiancée Sarah could not be consoled and committed suicide by hanging herself in a third floor room.

The pair may be dead but there are those who believe their restless spirits may still linger at the inn.

Numerous sightings of a ghost dubbed Harry have been reported for many years. Definitely not menacing, his spirit is extremely friendly to the ladies, and likes to play practical jokes. Nevertheless, there are some who refuse to go up the stairs, because you can *feel* "something" up there...

Several report a female wraith, called Sarah, who sits on the stairs. One night after closing a staffer rounded the corner and discovered a lady sitting on the stairs crying. The pale woman "didn't seem right" so the young man went to get the owner. When the pair returned she had vanished. Since all the doors were locked no one could have exited the building undetected.

After a 1969 fire, a passerby wanted to look inside to see the extent of the damage. To her amazement, she witnessed a transparent woman on the stairs.

These sightings are similar to the vast majority of hauntings where ghosts play out past memories. They appear oblivious to the environment, repeat the same actions in the same spot over and over, appear in the same clothing, and are seemingly unconscious.

The Wayside Inn at 101 W. Main Street sits on a spot with a long and rich history, which also helps.

Josiah Black erected the first building on the site as a "wayside" tavern and trading post in 1793. In 1806, Squire Munroe, and his four sons purchased Black's Tavern and added rooms to operate the place as a hostelry they called the Munroe House.

Other reputed ghosts at the inn are a man dressed in Revolutionary War-era garb in the upstairs rooms who stands next to the specter of a young girl. Another entity is the spirit of a long-ago traveler who stayed at the inn, had a heart attack in a second floor room, and died. His confused spirit still lingers.

Workers attest to unexplainable cold spots, females sometimes feel "something" touch their body as they walk through an empty room, and on one occasion, a case of beer floated in mid-air!

A former proprietor had high regard for the spirits who make the Wayside home. On occasion she felt queasy and would sense something behind her that sent chills up her spine. Even some patrons claimed the eerie sensation of a presence wafting past them that generated goose bumps.

Head Chef Jeff Ganey had an uncanny experience on a Mother's Day, one of the restaurant's busiest days.

When he opened at 6:00 A. M., he set about his preparations and headed to the walk-in refrigerator as three large sauté pans *flew* off the top of the convection oven. Ganey is adamant - flew, not just fell, underneath a large butcher-block table.

Knowing the bizarre incident he witnessed was out-of-this-world, he admonished the poltergeist to quit the unearthly high jinks on such a busy day. The ghost paid attention and behaved.

Another phenomenon is that when staffers open the restaurant in the morning from time to time they find the place settings rearranged.

As one worker pondered over paperwork, she heard the sound of heavy boots coming down the hallway outside her office. Normally accustomed to the odd goings-on, this time she ran for the comfort and safety of her co-worker, a petite woman, hardly capable of causing thundering footfalls.

Psychics and paranormal investigators agree the site is "active" and in all areas of the building. Photographs are full of orbs, bubble-like images considered to hold spirit energy, and electromagnetic field detectors register "positive."

Positively, you don't have to go looking for ghosts at the Wayside Inn - here they reach out to *you*.

Whimsy hill Studio
Fly Creek

3 miles north of Cooperstown is the hamlet of Fly Creek where Victorian portraitist Lady Ostapeck lives in a house spirited by its former owner. How "Lady O" landed in Fly Creek, where she is considered a "community treasure," is a mystery unto itself.

45 years ago, while working as a negative retoucher "with soul" in New York City, Lady O dreamed of living in the country. One evening she came upon a painting thrown in the trash and took it home for the frame. The painting showed a farmhouse and barn with maple trees and a horse. She hung the salvaged piece on the wall as inspiration in visualizing her dream, for Lady O knew then the power of the mind.

On a lark, she even advertised her desire - "Lady with horse seeks country home." Her ad received over 100 responses - and one in particular from Fly Creek.

Again, just for the fun of it, she drove up from Brooklyn to see the farm. When she pulled up to the property the scene was already familiar to her - the place closely resembled the painting that hung on the wall in her tiny apartment. She threw caution to the wind and bought the old farmhouse.

Now is when the real adventure began. How does a woman who lived and worked in the city make a living in the country? She relies on an invisible helper.

Victorian portraitist Lady Ostapeck lives in a house spirited by its former owner. (Photo by opera singer Phyllis Pancelli and courtesy of Lady Ostapeck).

Lady learned to persevere at an early age. Named after her mother who died when she was only five days old, she changed her name to "Lady" because she considered her given name unlucky. She survived the attack of an ax murderer because she credits her mother's spirit with diverting the crazed man away from her infant. So by the time Lady arrived in Fly Creek she was comfortable with putting her faith in spirits.

A Slovenian couple named Omagu previously owned the house. Mr. Omagu worked as a "wonderful" tailor, (Lady also had worked as a dressmaker). Now alone in her new home, or so she thought, when Lady needed something she felt led to what she looked-for.

She'd ask for guidance and quietly listened, listened for the "magic" to happen. The voice of Mrs. Omagu, the little old Slavic lady who raised cows and potatoes the old fashioned way, communicated with her and nudged her along toward a solution.

Lady felt the woman's ghost helped her and performed miracles. When feeling low a certain "change of air" would gently run by her and fill her with a sense of good cheer, "it was a blessing," Lady recalls.

At another low point Lady seriously considered giving up the country life and started to clean out the attic. Remarkably the Finnish native came upon a Finnish bible! How did a Finnish bible land in the attic of a Slovenian household? Lady discovered that Finnish sailors had taken refuge in the house and one of them must have left his holy book behind. Precisely what Lady needed to repair her spirit.

The unseen presence at the Whimsy Hill Studio is comforting and edifying. She leads Lady to see things in new ways. For instance, can't afford curtain rods? Sticks and strings will suffice.

Lady learned that there's a time for everything - as reinforced by the reading of the Finnish bible - thanks to the spirit of a little old Slovenian lady who helped a city girl learn how to live in the country - in a very big way.

One day in particular, remembered with crystal clarity, Lady felt drawn to the Salvation Army where an 80-year-old camera awaited to be brought back to life. Lady spotted the 5 x 7 Century view camera with red Russian leather bellows. Fitted with brass and made of rosewood, the camera "spoke" to Ostapeck. Reduced *that day* from $100 to $50, Lady plunked down her last $50.

At 42 years old, in her own imitable way, Lady embarked on a career as a portraitist. She relied heavily on her intuition, describing her sittings as séances and regarding Julia Margaret Cameron as her mentor, even though the 19th century soft-focus artist died decades ago.

Lady's enchanting work has been exhibited at various galleries in New York and Baltimore, and Finland and Great Britain, as well as being featured in *Modern Photography* and *Popular Photography*.

Recently Lady wanted to watch Pope John Paul II's funeral but knew she couldn't stay awake until 3:00 A.M. She went to bed and was awakened precisely at that hour by a loud screeching - the smoke alarm! Lady found her home engulfed in thick black smoke. She had left the hassock too close to the fire stove and it was smoldering. When she threw the piece outside it burst into flame.

Lady Ostapeck credits Mrs. Omagu, a devout Catholic, for watching over her - and waking her up in time to watch the pope's memorial service.

NORTH LAKE ROAD
Forestport

In their retreat, British forces traveled North Lake Road after their siege of Fort Stanwix.

Credible witnesses caught sight into an otherworldly realm and observed this historic, solemn departure being replayed in the early morning mist.

Many claim to hear the sounds of wounded soldiers moaning and the creak of wagon wheels as the phantom cortège travels slowly northward.

One of several historic markers in the region that conceals a rich haunted history.

OLD FORT HERKIMER, IN THE MOHAWK VALLEY, USED AS A PLACE OF REFUGE DURING REVOLUTIONARY WAR.

BUILT 1759

Old Fort Herkimer church in the Mohawk Valley served as a refuge during the Revolutionary War. Devastating raids drove surviving residents to retreat to fortified settlements. The first major raid on the valley came at German Flatts where the British burned all surrounding homes, barns, and mills, and drove off livestock. Patriots watched behind the garrison's walls as their homes and all their earthly possessions went up in flames. Is it any wonder that ghost investigators uncover evidence of ghostly presences?

HERKIMER CHURCH FORT
German Flatts

The 1756 Dutch Reformed Church sheltered colonists during the Revolutionary War and hosted a visit by General George Washington in 1783.

Located on Route 5S, the church's ancient burial ground holds the earthly remains of Indians, early settlers, and those who fought so bravely to preserve freedom in the struggle for independence.

During an investigation, ghost hunters from IMOVES, (Investigate, Manifestations, Orbs, Vortexes, Ecto, Spirits), videotaped floating images on the church's tower and unexplainable hovering lights and orbs in the cemetery.

One photo revealed an eerie, disembodied mustachioed face in the church window.[6]

Other paranormal surveyors experienced fresh battery failures and thermal indicators registered extreme temperature fluctuations, as much as 30 degrees.

A popular theory is that spirits draw energy from any available source in order to manifest so that's why batteries go dead, electronics malfunction, and "cold spots" exist at haunted places.

---

[5] View the photo on their website: www.imoves.net.

The Sherwood Inn
Greene

In 1803, Thomas Wattles built the Wattles Tavern offering meals and lodging for weary travelers.

1837 brought construction of the Chenango Canal and the need for a larger hotel to house the engineers and construction workers. When Wattles Tavern physically was moved to another location, the Chenango House went up on the Genesee Street site.

Tragedy struck in 1905 when fire consumed the Chenango and the new Sherwood Hotel rose from the ashes on the same foundation.

Again in 1962 fire destroyed most of the hotel's interior. Renovated and reopened, the hotel changed hands many times until 1995. The new owners restored the historic hotel to its former glory and renamed the place "The Sherwood Inn."

According to owner Pat Fragola, a female apparition, named "Rebecca," resides on the third-floor porch of the Victorian inn.

Years ago, Rebecca purportedly left Room 207 and jumped from a top floor balcony. Room 207 is haunted to this day since most sightings occur there, although some sense the female phantom in the basement, hallway and dining room.

An early hotel photo adorns a wall and looking closely you can see a shadowy figure, by all accounts, Rebecca's ghost captured on film for posterity.

HERKIMER COUNTY COURTHOUSE
Herkimer

The 1848 Herkimer County Courthouse and jail, made famous in *An American Tragedy* by Theodore Dreiser, housed Chester Gillette, the convicted murderer of Grace Brown.[7] The trial resulted in his conviction and ultimate execution in the electric chair in 1907.

Hanging from the gallows ended the life of many a criminal here. Part of the site's *haunted* history is that a filmy apparition of a man hanging with a noose around his neck is seen on occasion in the rear of the building.

[7] This writer witnessed Grace Brown's ghost hovering over Big Moose Lake where she was drowned. For the full account of the murder and subsequent sightings at Covewood Lodge see the author's *Adirondack Ghosts*.

BEARDSLEE CASTLE
Little Falls

Augustus Beardslee built the spooky looking castle on Route 5, between Little Falls and St. Johnsville, in the 1860s to replicate an Irish fortress. His son, Captain Guy Beardslee was born in the mansion and graduated West Point; he supervised the completion of the edifice, which ultimately became the region's social center.

Swiss stonemasons hand cut every stone quarried on the site that formed the structure and more than a mile of stone walls surround the park-like setting enhancing its eerie character.

Beardslee constructed a dam and power plant to furnish electricity, not only for his own farms, but also for the Village of St. Johnsville. "Street" lights turned on in the village on March 17, 1898.

According to historical records a small fort stood on the site about 1750, when the Mohawk Valley was wilderness. Legend has it that a tunnel led from the house into a hill where munitions were stored. During a raid on the fortress, Indians accidentally set off the gunpowder with their torches and were annihilated.

The burrow's entrance is in the basement and sealed by boulders. Some think the ghostly activity here could be restless Indian spirits. A stop on the Underground Railroad, perhaps slaves hid in the tunnel - their spirits lingering here as well.

A Beardslee son drowned nearby and the boy's spirit is often heard playing in the building, but is never found.

Legend says that Captain Beardslee's ghost roams the grounds at night carrying a lantern to light his way. Several auto accidents in the area have been attributed to Beardslee's ghost and his confounding light.

All manner of unexplained phenomena occurs at the creepy castle and is ascribed to a hefty number of ghosts.

"Pop" Anton M. Christensen purchased the property from Mrs. Beardslee and opened the mansion as a restaurant in 1941. He suffered from depression and ended up committing suicide by hanging. His frightening specter shows up dangling from a noose in the dark recess upstairs where he took his life.

After hours, staffers hear indiscernible voices and footsteps resound; orbs of light float through the rooms, lights are found on when turned off the night before, doors locked at night are unlocked in the morning, and an ungodly shriek, called the "Big Scream," resonates throughout the structure, its source unknown.

One employee shared that she suddenly felt icy cold and looked down to see a disembodied hand that looked like an x-ray image - she could see the bones.[8] Soon after, a co-worker observed a man dressed in a top hat and black suit standing in the same archway where the hand appeared; the "Abe Lincoln-like" image quickly dissipated.

A party guest captured the same dark apparition on film. Sightings of this entity have a long history and

---

Arthur Myers, *Ghostly American Places,* page 195.

those in the know identify him as Dominie Jake, a deacon accused of molesting children, according to the castle's chronicles.[9] The shamed clergyman purportedly hung himself in the underground passageway.

An odd cast of ghostly characters calls the castle home. There's the specter who sits in a wingback chair by the fireplace even though, in reality, there is no seating arranged there. A flaxen-haired wraith in a full-length dress frequents the ladies room. One worker observed a woman in a dressing gown carrying a bed tray up an invisible flight of stairs (before the remodel, a staircase existed there).

Once a diner peered into an upstairs banquet room and observed a foursome enjoying a candlelight dinner. Together with his server they investigated and found the room empty.

"Abigail" is yet another presence who supposedly served at the manor who choked and died. Her spirit speaks to the help whispering their names and giving them the heebie-jeebies.

Most of the mysterious activity takes place after hours. Not surprisingly, Beardslee Castle attracts a large number of ghost hunters. These serious investigators have recorded electronic voice phenomena (EVP). Their chilling recordings captured ghostly voices from the past whispering, "Why," and "Who is that person?"

As part of its *Haunted History* series, the History Channel filmed a segment at Beardslee Castle that premiered in 1999 and still airs in re-run.

---

[9] Ibid, page 191.

INDIAN CASTLE CHURCH
Little Falls

In 1769, Joseph Brant, noted Mohawk leader and brother of Molly Brant, Sir William Johnson's Mohawk mistress and mother of their eight children, donated the land and Sir William provided the funds to build a church for the Mohawks.

Incredibly, the tiny Indian mission church is the only surviving colonial building of any of the Mohawk or Iroquois castles[10] in New York State.

Owned and maintained by the Indian Castle Church Restoration and Preservation Society, the elegant 231-year-old church, rests on a knoll among pine trees and old tombstones. The white church, located on Route 5S, has long kept watch over Mohawk Valley travelers, and can be spotted from the New York State Thruway, the building of which obliterated many historic Indian sites during its construction.

According to Mohawk Valley Ghost Hunters, every one of their members literally feels touched by an unseen presence upon entering the spirited sanctuary - "something" invariably brushes against them.

In addition to making physical contact, ghost investigators captured white orbs of light, commonly thought to be spirit energy, with their infrared cameras.

---

[10] An Indian castle is a village protected by poles, stakes, or pickets.

The library's director has witnessed the ghost at the Huntington Memorial Library countless times.

HUNTINGTON MEMORIAL LIBRARY
Oneonta

Marie Bruni sees things most people don't. Gifted with clairvoyance, the ability to "see" with senses beyond the five we normally use, the Huntington Memorial Library's director has witnessed the book depository's ghost nearly every day for 22 years.

Solon and Harriet Huntington once lived in the Victorian structure that houses the present library on Chestnut Street. When the prominent couple died, son Henry inherited the property and later bequeathed the house to the city. He asked in return for the library to be renamed "The Huntington Memorial Library" in honor of his parents.

The regal-looking building still holds many Huntington possessions, including family portraits that adorn the walls along the stairwell. There are those who say Henry's eyes follow their every move, but the genuine ghost here is Harriet - no doubt about it.

Marie has witnessed the resident ghost countless times and first observed Harriet Huntington's specter the day of her interview. She has continued to perceive the woman's spirit ever since. The librarian's sensitivity to the spirits of the dead gives rare insight into their personalities and the reasons why they stay behind.

In Harriet's case her reason for lingering is that the woman simply loves her house and doesn't want to leave. Oddly though, her spirit did take leave once and stayed away for two years. Marie has no idea why she left or where Harriet went in the meantime, but her spirit returned and at times, is in rare form.

Harriet's feelings run the gamut of emotions. Initially sad over the building's disrepair she gets upset when the place is refurbished. Just like most living mortals, Harriet doesn't care for change and she shows her displeasure.

Her spirit will act out by taking things and moving them, a mischievous practice that confounds the staff. Once an expensive library catalog went missing for days but finally showed up standing open on top of a file cabinet in plain sight.

Although happy with the environment, Harriet's mischief is her way of reminding everyone from time to time that the library is first and foremost *her* home.

The library director's office occupies a former servant's bedroom. One time when she returned to work after a close friend's death, Marie discovered a live blackbird in her office. The office remained locked the entire time and there was no way the bird could have gained entry. Another odd thing about the incident was the absence of bird droppings.

Symbolically birds represent the spirits of the dead, but this is one instance that Marie finds unexplainable. The blackbird simply flew away when she opened the window.

Over the years, even patrons have witnessed Harriet's translucent apparition and, although startling, they gladly accept the presence of the benevolent ghost.

ONEONTA HISTORICAL SOCIETY
Oneonta

Oneonta's historical society is housed in the city's oldest commercial brick building at 183 Main Street. Formerly Laskaris' luncheonette and confectionary shop, the corner structure accommodates a ghost according to Mark Simonson, the "City of the Hills" historian.

About a century ago, a teenage boy died accidentally in the building's elevator shaft and his spirit still lingers in the basement.

Marie Bruni, the Director of the Huntington Memorial Library, possesses a "sixth sense." She receives images and messages by "seeing" with what is commonly called the "third eye."

Marie has perceived the boy's presence and says he doesn't realize he's dead; his spirit is "full of life," so to speak.

The teenager thinks he's still a flesh and blood energetic youth and continues to live out his life in another realm where time is measured differently than in our dimension. The librarian says that even though the boy has been deceased for decades, to him it's been but a mere moment and he has yet to absorb the reality of his situation.

(*National Park Service Photo.*)

The Battle of Oriskany, fought on August 6, 1777, to defend Fort Stanwix, is described as one of the bloodiest engagements of the Revolutionary War. Some feel the battle is still being fought in an otherworldly realm.

ORISKANY BATTLEFIELD
Oriskany

In the late 18th century, the British commanded Colonel Barry St. Leger to enter the Mohawk Valley from west to east and destroy all the settlements along the river. The colonel decided he'd attack Fort Stanwix before proceeding down river.

General Nicholas Herkimer organized a force of 800 men against St. Leger's troops. Upon hearing of Herkimer's advance, the opposition set a trap in a swampy gorge west of Oriskany Creek.

As unsuspecting American troops crossed the bog and marched up the ravine, the British attacked. Brutal combat ensued, and in spite of heavy losses, the enemy retreated.

The ambush left Herkimer mortally wounded - over half his troops and Oneida allies were dead, wounded or captured. The Battle of Oriskany, fought on August 6, 1777, is described as one of the bloodiest engagements of the Revolutionary War yet is considered a significant turning point in the struggle.

Battlefields are notoriously haunted places because of the intense emotion generated during conflict. Some visitors who walk the ravine sense they are not alone.

Neighbors often hear the cries and screams of spectral men, and gunfire; motorists notice strange sparks of light and orbs floating in the woods - all chilling anomalies revealing the lasting energy of war.

(National Park Service Photo)

At Fort Stanwix, a dedicated spirit carries on his chores from beyond the grave evidenced by the unexplained cleanly swept floors and inexplicable supply of newly chopped wood occasionally found there.

Fort Stanwix
Rome

The site of Fort Stanwix was an Oneida "carrying place," an Iroquois Nation portage used to bridge the waterways. Built in 1758, the stronghold safeguarded the Mohawk Valley's major thoroughfare during the French and Indian War.

During the American Revolution, British military forces were driven back while attempting to capture the fort. American militiamen and Oneida allies tried to aid Fort Stanwix but were ambushed at Oriskany.

A colorful chapter in "Old Glory's" history occurred when the defenders of Fort Stanwix decided to fashion a flag to fly over the fort. For the blue, they used a cloak captured from a British officer, regular army shirts served as the white stripes and stars, and the red material came from a woman's flannel petticoat.

Much like the ghostly goings-on at several other ancient New York forts, spectral soldiers in period dress materialize in various places throughout the garrison. At sunrise, musical strains from phantom fifes and drums occasionally echo from the fortress.

Other phantom fare includes the disembodied sound of a woman weeping and some visitors allege to have spotted the spirit of a one-legged man sitting in the barracks.

ORCHARD HALL
Sauquoit

"Julia" is the specter who resides at 2955 Oneida Street. Said to be the victim of an errant bullet, owner Sharon Puleo witnessed the woman's luminescent apparition two years after she and her husband purchased the 19th century building.

Sharon could hardly believe her eyes as she watched the white figure come down the stairs, go into the kitchen, come out and go back up the stairs.

The couple had heard rumors about ghosts and haunting activity at the place but kept the thought on the back burner while they breathed new life into the historic restaurant and bowling hall.

Built around 1843, Orchard Hall most likely was a stop on the Underground Railroad. Down in the cellar, open passageways could have sheltered slaves passing through Oneida, a main traffic route. Some say Julia, a former owner, actively assisted the freedom finders and one psychic detected the presence of a black man wearing old-fashioned clothes in the basement. Workers are reluctant to go down there because they always get the feeling that someone is watching them.

Julia's ghost primarily dwells in one of the nine upstairs bedrooms where her apparition once sat rocking in a chair.

Two friends stayed overnight in the room and rushed out at the crack of dawn without a minute of sleep. During the night, doors kept opening, and unexplainable noises and footsteps kept the musicians awake all night. Sharon forgot to tell them about Julia.

Passersby often claim to see a light go on in the room and a female silhouette standing at the window. It is surmised that Julia gave up the ghost, so to speak, in that bedroom.

Psychic mediums described Julia as in her thirties and perceive her wearing Victorian dress. The appearance of an authentically garbed 19th century woman traipsing through the dining room puzzled Gary Puleo when one of the diners expressed an appreciation for the performance as they supped. "A nice touch," the patron quipped. Needless to say, the Puleos had not hired any such person, but felt certain they knew who had strutted her stuff.

While contractors were installing a new heating system during the night, they heard someone upstairs banging about the kitchen. They assumed Gary made the noise and fully expected the owner to come down and greet them. He never did.

The next day when the workman questioned Gary, well, you know the rest... Not Gary, or anyone else occupied the building the night before - no *living* soul that is.

Other curious after hour oddities are staffers sometimes hear the sound of phantom bowlers and detect the pungent odor of cigar smoke. At times the scent of perfume is present. "Cold spots" are commonly reported in the ladies room and one female patron got chills when she heard a woman cough when the customer *knew* she was alone in the restroom.

Fort Klock
St. Johnsville

Located on Route 5, on the north bank of the Mohawk River, Johannes Klock constructed the L-shaped, story and half stone house in 1750 where settlers sought refuge during the French and Indian and Revolutionary Wars.

The National Historic Landmark, fully restored and open as a museum, is an excellent example of a mid-18th century fur trading post and fortified house structure.

During the War for Independence, captured and wounded British soldiers and their Indian allies were held prisoner in Fort Klock's cellar until they could be transported to another location. The men were secured to the wall by chains, which remain intact to this day, as do the bloodstains forever defacing the stone floor.

One Brit, who had been shot and sustained a serious injury, sat chained to the cold stone wall and perished during a frigid winter night.

Unable to bury the body in the frozen earth, his remains were burned in the field, along with several other comrades who had fallen in battle.

It is surmised that because he has no grave or stone marker to commemorate his death, the soldier's spirit is trapped in the cellar where he died. Late at night his moans emanate from the deathly cold cellar.

COMMANDER'S HOUSE
Syracuse

James Lynch built a house on 100-acres in Onondaga County when he came from Ireland to escape the potato famine in 1835. His wife died soon after they arrived.

In 1941, the Army Air Corps built the Mattydale Bomber Base around the property and Lynch's sturdy old farmhouse sheltered the families for a string of base commanders at the re-christened Hancock Field.

Some residents heard the floor creak, footsteps, strains of music, and a woman weeping when no one else occupied the house. Lights turned on without benefit of human hand and missing items turned up in strange places days later. Inhabitants never felt alone.

Cats, known to be sensitive to the unseen, acted weird and crept under beds where they slept, a behavior totally out of character.

Some officers and their spouses observed a furtive shadow pass through the rooms or float up the stairs. At times the figure assumed the definite form of a man with long gray hair and dressed in a cape. One worker observed a woman wearing a housedress peering out the window when no woman lived in the house.

When the Air Force moved out in 1984 the city of Syracuse took possession, running the property as a municipal airport and renting out the house. Today's tenants deny the presence of any gray-haired ghosts or spectral haus fraus.

ENGINE CO. 18
Syracuse

Before the brick building at 176 West Seneca Turnpike housed the Robert Cecile Community Center, the site gave shelter to Engine Co. 18. Many firemen who worked, slept and served there heard the footsteps.

Although no one would definitely admit to ghosts at the firehouse, someone, or some*thing*, walked about the upstairs station house dormitory. Firemen downstairs would hear the footsteps and call out or go to investigate. Immediately the noise would stop.

One night, as a firefighter slept in his bed, he awoke with a start to the sound of footsteps. As he looked around he observed a figure at the top of the stairs. When the fireman got up and approached the form, it vanished. The only other person in the station slept soundly downstairs.

The firefighter returned to bed and before he nodded off for a second time, he noticed the figure standing at the top of the stairs again.

Some concluded that the vigilant presence was a deceased crew member watching over his brothers. Since the building went up in 1927 over a historic Revolutionary War and Native American trail, perhaps its location has something to do with the shade.

Now that the firehouse is a senior citizens center no one hears the footsteps anymore.

LANDMARK THEATER
Syracuse

Architect Thomas W. Lamb described his 1928 Loew's State Theatre as "European, Byzantine, and Romanesque." Opened near the close of the "roaring twenties," the theatre presented famous stage acts and first-run movies. When the stock market crashed, the show palace offered a temporary respite from the despair of the depression.

As theatergoers were ushered into the main lobby they delighted in the glow of a Louis Comfort Tiffany chandelier just like the one designed for Cornelius Vanderbilt's mansion, and were awed by the theater's grand murals. Musicians, seated in the gallery located over the front doors, serenaded the crowd during intermissions.

Decorated in rich reds and golds, the showplace walls dripped with lavish embellishments throughout. A 1,400-pipe Wurlitzer organ offered the exotic tones of glockenspiel, marimba, bird whistles, hoof beats and surf sounds.

Unfortunately, like so many other great movie palaces, attendance steadily declined. By 1975, it seemed inevitable that the pride of Syracuse would fall victim to the wrecker's ball.

Luckily, in 1977 a group of concerned citizens formed the Syracuse Area Landmark Theatre, or SALT. When the group began restoring the showplace the volunteers and staff could never have imagined that they would breathe new life into long-gone theatergoers.

In the upper balcony, employees encountered a pale young female dressed entirely in white. When the ushers politely asked her to leave the area she faded from their sight. Psychics intuit that she is the spirit of a woman named Clare whose husband worked at the theater; she spent all her life longing to perform on stage.

Her ghost has inspired a children's book and a theater show, though no one really knows her true story. Clare's specter is occasionally spotted standing before a gilded mirror brushing her hair and she's been known to call the stagehands by name.

Another spirit haunting the palace is a former electrician. Oscar Rau's ghost has been observed near the light board.

Many have witnessed a mysterious blue light throughout the theatre but especially near the banister running along the back of the auditorium, in the catwalk access hallway, and on the stairs leading to the downstairs dressing room.

Some intuitives claim that the Red Room still tingles with the passionate energies of ghostly players involved in a violent love triangle.

The basement is off limits to the timid as is the Walnut Room - both areas are plagued with inexplicable cold spots.

Today, the theater continues its restoration and fundraising efforts, while offering the Syracuse area a full schedule of performances by the living - and the dead.

PARKE S. AVERY HISTORICAL HOUSE
Syracuse

Successful "salt baron," Parke S. Avery built his Italian style villa at 419 N. Salina Street in the mid 19th century atop a former burial ground.

One hundred years later in 1952, the last Avery to inhabit the house fell to his death down a staircase. Locals felt that a malevolent force may have pushed him since so many Avery men met their death by falls.

When the Preservation Association of Central New York occupied the property, staffers often heard footsteps upstairs even though the floors were carpeted.

David J. Pitkin writes in *Ghosts of the Northeast*, that a psychic intuited the male presence to be the forsaken love of one of the daughters who died from influenza. His spirit stays behind in hopes of a reunion.

There may be more than one entity in the house. A medium claims that the disgruntled spirit of a mortician is mourning the money he lost when the Avery family used another undertaker to perform their funerals. He's out big bucks because the preliminary planning for the family's demise went unpaid.

Once, to their great astonishment, two workers observed a pair of trousers, nothing more, traipsing up the sidewalk. Simultaneously an unusually strong wind gust blew through the office and created a supernatural whirlwind of papers.

*Split Rock Quarry - where the specters
of accident victims still roam.*

SPLIT ROCK QUARRY
Syracuse

On April 18, 1918, an industrial accident at Split Rock Quarry just west of Syracuse took the lives of fifty men and injured one hundred others.

In an effort to keep up with wartime demands, Solvay Processing Company operated 24 hours a day mining and processing ore and extracting minerals vital to the production of picric acid, a bitter, toxic, yellow crystal used to make TNT.

During the nightshift, a gear overheated sparking a fire that rapidly spread and caused an explosion that took the lives of so many. Fifteen victims were never identified and they were buried in a common grave.

More than eighty years after the plant blew up, the specters of the fifteen dead men were spotted roaming the ledges and standing on the ruined rock crusher of the old quarry.

Their apparitions glowed a ghostly yellow-green - a spectral residue of the effects of the picric acid that once stained their skin chartreuse.

Syracuse City Hall may harbor a specter.

SYRACUSE CITY HALL
Syracuse

Fortress-like Syracuse City Hall is evocative of European town halls, yet Albany's City Hall provided the inspiration for this Onondaga limestone building.

Architect Charles E. Colton's structure features turrets, a hipped roof with steeply pitched dormers, an arcaded entrance porch, and a 165-foot bell tower that spurred political controversy.

Initially a smaller City Hall stood on the site and the bell tower atop this building served an important part of life in the city. The bell rang out to summon volunteer firefighters and pealed to commemorate both sad and happy occasions.

The brass bell was taken from the old City Hall and temporarily installed in a makeshift tower on Columbus Circle until the time came to install the bell in Colton's tower. Colton stubbornly refused to deface his tower by adding mechanical equipment.

Mayor Kirk felt strongly that the bell belonged in the new tower and removed Colton from the project. Colton's assistant, Frederick A. Whelan, oversaw the final stages of construction, including the installation of the bell.

Not everyone agreed about the importance of the bell and expressed their displeasure at the ballot box in 1891. Mayor Kirk lost his re-election, some say, over the bell tower controversy.

The old bell functioned in the new tower for nearly 50 years, ringing for the last time on Armistice Day, 1939. The city melted down the controversial bell for use by Allied troops in World War II.

No bell rang again in Syracuse until 1987 when the Rotary Club donated an electronic carillon. A brass-plated aluminum bell was also installed for show.

Did this colorful episode incite the strange goings-on that plague City Hall?

After hours, a certain imp likes to ride the elevators. A former maintenance worker claimed to hear an elevator running after midnight. She had just checked the building so she knew no one else occupied the Gothic structure.

Automated since 1970, the elevators frequently malfunction. Pushing a button does not guarantee arrival at that floor. Is the problem a phantom's ploy to keep individuals from their desired destination? Technicians, constantly called in to repair the errant contraptions, never find anything out of order and are at a loss to explain the problem.

Doors open on their own and, in the basement, the wraith's chilly epicenter, disembodied footsteps resound down the stairs, (doesn't the scamp like to take the elevator?). Maybe it's Charles Colton's spirit still stewing over his compromised bell tower or Mayor Kirk bemoaning his lost election.

Some workers feel the culprit is the spirit of a long-dead inmate housed in the building when it served as a jail.

Whoever it is, the unseen presence gives workers the willies.

FIRST PRESBYTERIAN CHURCH
Utica

Robert Mackinon, a well educated and much admired Scottish immigrant, made his fortune partnering in the milling industry in Cohoes and Little Falls. In 1898, he moved his family north for greater cultural opportunities and erected the greatest home ever built in Utica.

In June 1910, Mackinon hosted a grand wedding for one of his daughters; the 700 guests who attended the gala were spellbound by thousands of flowers. On the contrary, by the close of the year, the businessman suffered a reversal of fortune and had lost everything.

Mackinon endured further trials. Shortly after her wedding the newlywed daughter and her husband, who owned approximately one-third of the island, moved to Jamaica where she died shortly thereafter. Another daughter mysteriously disappeared in 1916 and never re-emerged. A third daughter died in the charity ward of a New York City hospital and his reclusive son lived out his life in a veteran's hospital.

Mackinon's mansion languished for years and the First Presbyterian Church eventually acquired the property.

Mohawk Valley Ghost Hunters with their infrared cameras and other high-tech equipment were called in to check out some paranormal activity at the house of worship. The group detected an "active presence," and filmed darting globules of light in a dark hallway and the church sanctuary.

What's more is that there are those who have directly experienced some remarkable goings-on at the site. Incredibly, on two different occasions, a church secretary and a burly workman, quite shaken by the ghost's appearance on the grand staircase, sighted the full-bodied apparition of a woman wearing a floor-length ivory gown.

Visitors to the third floor ballroom felt a backwards push. There's no proof as to who is doing the shoving - we can only speculate.

Who would have thought that the blessed family who held so much promise would face such demise? Possibly it's their lonely spirits who have returned to recapture happier days.

Another inexplicable incident occurred while the church custodian attended to his duties; he misstepped and began to plummet off his ladder. Suddenly, unseen hands caught him and prevented his fall. *This* spirit was far from pushy, or perhaps the divine interceded to avert the fall...

CENTRAL NEW YORK GHOST TOURS

Cooperstown Candlelight Ghost Tours...

...Illumine the village's eerie history.
Hear about our haunted houses.
Learn more about our ghostly sightings.
For reservations & information call:
(607) 547-8070 or e-mail: bmark@telenet.net.

Mohawk Valley Ghost Hunters

Walk Indian burial grounds, old castles, and other
haunted sites including Beardslee Manor.
For info e-mail: MVGHunters@aol.com.

Things That Go Bump In The Night

The Farmer's Museum in Cooperstown presents a
guided tour of the village & guides share stories of the
area's hauntings in the autumn.
Call (607) 547-1450 or (888) 547-1450.

Acknowledgments

There was certain magic in researching this book. One story led to the next with ease and serendipity. Every individual contacted had something interesting to offer and in many cases I felt like I was talking with a long lost friend. I also feel I made some new ones...

I'd like to thank the following folks for their time and willingness to share with me their knowledge of Central New York hauntings.

A sincere "thank you" goes to Steven Best, First Presbyterian Church, Utica; Marie Bruni, Director, Huntington Memorial Library, Oneonta; Robert Brzozowski, President, Oneonta Historical Society; Katherine Collett, Archivist, Hamilton College, Clinton; Marie Curpier, The Inn at Hickory Grove, Cooperstown; Joan Haskell, Farmer's Museum, Cooperstown; Mike Henrici, Tunnicliff Inn, Cooperstown; Barabra Lyon and Rachel Purcell, The Otesago, Cooperstown; Bruce Markusen, Cooperstown Candlelight Ghost Tours; Lady Ostapeck, Whimsy Hill Studios, Fly Creek; Sharon Puleo, Orchard Hall Restaurant and Bowling Hall, Sauquoit; Elsie Schiellack, Cooperstown Chamber of Commerce; Mark Simonson, Historian, City of Oneonta; Tara Sumner, Director, The Smithy-Pioneer Gallery, Cooperstown; Sue Ulrich, Dodge-Pratt-Northam Art & Community Center, Boonville; and Robert Tegart, Clinton Historical Society.

BIBLIOGRAPHY

Atwell, Jim. "A story of portable ghosts." *The Cooperstown Crier*; October 17, 2002.

Cooper, James Fenimore. *The Legends and Traditions of a Northern County.* G.P. Putnam's Sons; 1921.

Ellis, Suzanne M. "Ghosts Said To Lurk In Region." *The Post-Standard*; October 31, 2004.

Hauck, Dennis William. *The National Directory of Haunted Places.* Penguin Books; 1996.

Jones, Louis C., *Things That Go Bump In The Night.* Syracuse University Press; 1983.

Macken, Lynda Lee. *Empire Ghosts.* Black Cat Press; 2004.

Myers, Arthur. *The Ghostly Register,* Contemporary Books; 1986.

Nayor, Ella. "Halloween haunts." *Binghamton Press & Sun-Bulletin*; October 25, 2003.

Novak, Peter. "Ghosts, Poltergeists, and the Lost Secret of Death." *GHOST! Magazine*; February 2004.

Pierce, Frederic. "New York's Haunted Havens." *The Post-Standard*; October 26, 2003.

Pitkin, David J. *Ghosts of the Northeast.* Aurora Publications; 2002.

Reilly, Jim. "Spirits Among Us." *Syracuse Herald American*; October 29, 1995.

Seely, Hart. "Workers Say Inn Is Haunted Every Day, Not Just Halloween." *The Post-Standard*; October 31, 2001.

Simonson, Mark. "Will's power created Roberson center." *The Daily Star*; December 20, 2003.

Smitten, Susan. *Ghost Stories of New York State.* Ghost House Books; 2004.

Sorensen, Erik. "Ghost hunters scour Inn for troubled
  Spirits." *The Citizen*; (date unknown).
Walden, Justin. "Spooky Stories." *Binghamton Press & Sun-
  Bulletin*; October 29, 2002.
Webster, Dennis. "Ghost Hunting Virgin." *GHOST!
  Magazine*; Issue 2, 2005.

Websites

Central NY Ghost Hunters: www.gotghosts.org
Farmer's Museum: www.farmersmuseum.org
Ghosts of Beardslee Castle: www.beardsleecastle.com
Ghost Seekers Inc. of CNY: www.cnyghosts.com
Hyde Hall: www.hydehall.org
IMOVES: www.imoves.net
James Fenimore Cooper Society: www.oneonta.edu
Landmark Theatre: www.landmarktheatre.org
Lorenzo State Historic Site: www.lorenzony.org
National Park Service: www.cr.nps.gov
New York State Division of Military & Naval Affairs:
  www.dmna.state.ny.us
New York State Parks: www.nysparks.state.ny.us
Paul Kessler Books: paulkesslerbooks.com
The Otesaga: www.otesaga.com
Roberson Museum & Science Center: www.roberson.org
Rome Sentinel: www.rny.com
The Smithy-Pioneer Gallery: www.thesmithypioneer.com
Southern Adirondack Trail: www.adirondack.org
Syracuse City Hall: www.syracusethenandnow.net
Syracuse Ghost Hunters: pages.prodigy.net/kas9865/
Three Rivers, Hudson, Mohawk, Schoharie:
  www.threerivershms.com

BLACK CAT PRESS...

Post Office Box 1218, Forked River, New Jersey 08731
Visit our website: www.lyndaleemacken.com

...Publishes **13** _Scary_ titles by _Lynda Lee Macken!_

ADIRONDACK GHOSTS
Haunted Places in New York's North Country
ISBN 0-9700718-1-7 ~ $7.95

ADIRONDACK GHOSTS II
More Haunted Places in New York's North Country
ISBN 0-9700718-6-8 ~ $8.95

EMPIRE GHOSTS
New York State's Haunted Landmarks
ISBN 0-9700718-8-4 ~ $8.95

LEATHERSTOCKING GHOSTS
Haunted Places in Central New York
ISBN 0-9755244-2-9 ~ $9.95

HAUNTED LONG ISLAND
Ghosts & Haunted Places in New York's
Nassau & Suffolk Counties
ISBN 0-9755244-0-2 ~ $8.95

GHOSTLY GOTHAM
New York City's Haunted History
ISBN 0-9700718-4-1 ~ $9.95

HAUNTED HISTORY OF STATEN ISLAND
Mysterious People & Places in
New York's Richmond County
ISBN 0-9700718-0-9 ~ $7.95

GHOSTS OF THE GARDEN STATE
Haunted Places in New Jersey
ISBN 0-9700718-2-5~ $7.95

GHOSTS OF THE GARDEN STATE II
ISBN 0-9700718-7-6 ~ $8.95

GHOSTS OF THE GARDEN STATE III
More Haunted Places in New Jersey
ISBN 0-9755244-1-0 ~ $8.95

HAUNTED CAPE MAY
ISBN 0-9700718-5-X ~ $8.95

HAUNTED SALEM & BEYOND
Witchcraft, Commerce, Seafarers & Slaves
ISBN 0-9700718-3-3 ~ $7.95

HAUNTED BALTIMORE
Charm City's Spirits
ISBN 0-9700718-9-2 ~ $8.95

All books available at most bookstores and on-line,
or send $1.50 postage for <u>each</u> title ordered to:

BLACK CAT PRESS
Post Office Box 1218
Forked River, New Jersey 08731
Visit our website: www.lyndaleemacken.com